SEC 302 IPC- SUPREME COURT'S LATEST LEADING CASE LAWS

CASE NOTES- FACTS- FINDINGS OF APEX COURT JUDGES & CITATIONS

JAYPRAKASH BANSILAL SOMANI

Dedicated

To

All the Past & Present Judges of the Supreme Court of India.

Salute to their wisdom.

Salute to their interpretation of Law.

Salute to their elaborative judgement writing.

Contents

Preface

Dear Learned Advocates of the Trial Courts, Session Courts, High Courts, Supreme Court & Individuals,

I am very delighted to provide you a book on 'SEC 302 IPC' - Supreme Court of India's Latest Leading Case Laws'.

In this book you will get...

1. Name of the Case i. e. Cause title

2.Relevant Sections discussed in the case

3. Hon'ble Judges/Coram of the case

4.Number of PDF Pages in Original Judgement of the case

5. All available Citations of the case

6. Case Note with appeal allowed/ dismissed or disposed off

7. Facts of the case

8. Hon'ble Apex Court's findings, while dismissing/allowing or disposing the appeal

9. Ratio Decidendi if any.

My special thanks to Manupatra, because of their web portal I can compile this book in well manner. I am also thankful to Notion Press to support me to publish & market this book throughout the Country. Thanks to my Juniors, Advocate Colleagues & Insolvency Professional Colleagues to support me in this venture.

Miss Devpriya Shah has helped me a lot to compile this book.

I hope this book will add some value addition in the wealth of your legal knowledge. Your positive feedbacks will boost me to compile/ write further books & negative feedbacks will improve my skills. Kindly send your valuable feedbacks by email.

Thanks with Regards,

Jayprakash B. Somani

Advocate, Supreme Court of India

Email: jaysomani64@gmail.com

Web Site:www.jayprakashsomani.com

Call: 8384051134, 9322188701, 8459194576

Acknowledgements

Printed & Published by
Notion Press
No. 8, 3rd Cross Street,
CIT Colony, Mylapore,
Chennai, Tamil Nadu- 600004

Managed by
Jayprakash Somani Advocates & Solicitors
Law Firm for Supreme Court of India
Delhi Office
257 C, Pocket 1, Mayur Vihar Phase 1, Delhi 110091.
Call 8384051134, 9322188701, 8459194576
Supreme Court Chamber
312, 3rd Floor, M. C. Setalvad Block, In front of 'D' Gate, Bhagwan Das
Road, Supreme Court of India, New Delhi 110001
Contact: 8459194576, 9811011747
www.jayprakashsomani.com

Books are available online in India
1. Notion Press:https://notionpress.com/author/jayprakash_somani
2. Amazon:https://www.amazon.in/s?k=jayprakash+somani
3. Flipkart:https://www.flipkart.com/search?q=Jayprakash%20Somani
Books are available online at International Market
4. Amazon International: https://www.amazon.com/
s?k=jayprakash+somani
5. Amazon United Kingdom: https://www.amazon.co.uk/
s?k=jayprakash+somani
6. E-Books/Kindle edition at National & International Level:
https://www.amazon.in/s?k=jaypraksh+somani

CHAPTER ONE

Rajesh Prasad Vs. The State of Bihar and Ors., 2022

Hon'ble Judges/Coram:

L. Nageswara Rao, B.R. Gavai and B.V. Nagarathna, JJ.

Equivalent Citation: 2022(1)RCR(Criminal)681, MANU/SC/0022/2022

Relevant Section: Sections 34, 120B and 302 of the Indian Penal Code, 1860

Number of Pages in the Original Judgment: 18

Case Note:

Criminal - Acquittal - Offences allegedly under Sections 34, 120B, 302of the Indian Penal Code, 1860 (IPC) - Respondents convicted by Trial Court - High Court reversed conviction and thereby Respondent Accused acquitted - Hence, the present appeal - Whether the High Court was justified in reversing the judgment of conviction and sentence awarded by Trial Court?

Brief Facts:

The present appeals were directed by the Informant (PW-7) challenging High Court's judgment setting aside conviction and order of sentence, and consequently acquitting all the Accused. Prior to this, Trial Court had convicted the Respondents. Appellants contended that High Court was not right in setting aside conviction since evidence of relevant witnesses contended that the same would clearly establish the guilt of the Accused beyond reasonable doubt. It was contended that High Court has not appreciated the case of the Appellant herein in its proper perspective. Hence, the present appeal.

Held, while partly allowing the Appeal:

i. Fast Track Court failed to appreciate the evidence of PWs-1, 3, 4 and 7 in their proper perspective and has further failed to recognise the fact that PW-7/the Appellant herein did not at all support the case of the prosecution although he was the informant and hence, erroneously convicted the Accused and sentenced two of them with death penalty and the third Accused with imprisonment for life. High Court wasjustified in reversing the judgment and order of conviction passed by the Fast-Track Court.

ii. As also noted, the State has not filed any appeal against the judgment and order of acquittal passed by the High Court.

iii. Having re-appreciated the evidence of the witnesses, the High Court was justified in reversing the judgment of conviction and sentencing.

iv. Further, the High Court has stated this to be a fit case for initiating proceedings of perjury against the Appellant (PW-7) herein. Trial Court to initiate proceedings of perjury against the Appellant herein. Appeals allowed in part.

CHAPTER TWO

Jaikam Khan Vs. The State of Uttar Pradesh, 2021

Hon'ble Judges/Coram:

L. Nageswara Rao, B.R. Gavai and B.V. Nagarathna, JJ.

Equivalent Citation: 2022(1)ADJ292, MANU/SC/1259/2021

Relevant Section: Sections 34, 302 of the Indian Penal Code, 1860

Number of Pages in the Original Judgment: 18

Case Note:

Criminal - Conviction - Death Sentence - Sections 34, 302 of the Indian Penal Code, 1860 (IPC) - Impugned judgment by High Court set aside the order of conviction in respect of Accused No. 2 - Present appellants aggrieved by order of acquittal of original Accused No. 2 - Whether Trial Court and High Court erred in acquitting A-2 while convicting other Accused in similar set of circumstances?

Brief Facts:

The present appeal was preferred by Appellants challenging their conviction when in the similar circumstances Accused No. 2 was acquitted. Appellants were awarded capital punishment. It was contended by Appellants that prosecution had failed to prove case beyond reasonable doubt and hence conviction as directed liable to be set aside.

Held, while allowing the Appeal:

i. The prosecution has failed to bring home the guilt of the Accused beyond reasonable doubt and however, the trial court and the High Court were expected to exercise a greater degree of scrutiny, care and circumspection while directing the Accused to be hanged till death.

ii. If the arrest of the Accused No. 2 was from a public place, was the arrest of the Accused Nos. 1, 3 and 4 from any other place than the place from where the Accused No. 2 was apprehended. If according to the High Court, there is no independent witness of her arrest, is there any independent witness for arrest of Accused Nos. 1, 3 and 4. It is the duty of the prosecution to prove the case beyond reasonable doubt.

iii. The prosecution has utterly failed to prove the case beyond reasonable doubt. The conviction and death sentence imposed on the Accused is totally unsustainable in law.

CHAPTER THREE

Jayamma and Ors. Vs. State of Karnataka, 2021

Hon'ble Judges/Coram:

N.V. Ramana, C.J.I., Surya Kant and Aniruddha Bose, JJ.

Equivalent Citation: 2021(223)AIC95, AIR2021SC2399, 2021 (117) ACC 323, 2021 (3) ALT (Crl.) 212 (A.P.), 2021(2)BomCR(Cri)542, 2021CriLJ2900, 2021(2)Crimes246(SC), 2021(3)J.L.J.R.76, 2021(3)JKJ102[SC], 2021(4)KarLJ177, 2021(3)KCCR2081, 2021(2)MLJ(Crl)550, 2021 (2) MWN (CR.) 356, 2021(2)N.C.C.575, 2021(II)OLR88, 2021(3)PLJR68, 2021(3)RCR(Criminal)50, (2021)6SCC213, MANU/SC/0347/2021

Relevant Section: Section 34 and 302 of the Indian Penal Code, 1860; Section 378 of the Code of Criminal Procedure 1973

Number of Pages in the Original Judgment: 12

Case Note:

Criminal - Conviction - Sections 34 and 302 of the Indian Penal Code, 1860 (IPC) - High Court vide impugned finding reversed Appellants' acquittal- Trial Court had acquitted Appellant on the ground of absence of corroborative evidence - High Court however held otherwise holding that dying declaration was clinching enough to prove the guilt - Hence the present appeal - Whether the High Court erred in reversing the findings of the trial Court in exercise of its powers Under Section 378 of the Code of Criminal Procedure? - Whether the prosecution successfully established that the deceased died a homicidal death at the hands of the Appellants?

Brief Facts:

The parties in the present case are closely related. The case of the prosecution is that there was a long-standing animosity between the families of Appellant No. 1 and deceased. In connection therewith, a quarrel took place. Appellants allegedly doused the deceased in kerosene and set her on fire. Specific roles were attributed to all the Appellants in respect thereto. Arrest was made. Appellants pleaded not guilty and claimed trial. During the course of trial, several prosecution witnesses turned hostile. Son of the deceased, put forward an alternative chain of events wherein he claimed that the deceased committed suicide because she couldn't bear the fact that her son was arrested and sent to jail for beating husband of the 1st Appellant. Since it was not in dispute that deceased died due to burn injuries, the crucial question before the trial Court was whether the death was suicidal or homicidal. Considering the mitigating circumstances such as testimonies of the hostile witnesses, nature of burn injuries of the victim, and the lack of any corroborative evidence, trial Court acquitted the Appellants. High Court in appeal reversed the findings and held that the evidence consisting of dying declaration was clinching and sufficient to bring the guilt home. Hence, the present appeal.

Held, while allowing the Appeal:

i. The judgment of the trial court cannot be set aside merely because the High Court finds its own view more probable, save where the judgment of the trial court suffers from perversity or the conclusions drawn by it were impossible if there was a correct reading and analysis of the evidence on record. Unless High Court finds that there is complete misreading of the material evidence which has led to miscarriage of justice, the view taken by the trial court which can also possibly be a correct view, need not be interfered with.

ii. The Additional Sessions Judge extensively examined the entire evidence and after reaching to the conclusion that all the witnesses of the motive or the occurrence have resiled and declared hostile, he was left with the residuary question to decide as to whether the death was suicidal or homicidal. He, thereafter, considered the dying declaration threadbare and critically analysed the statements of the police officer and the doctor. The factors like (i) interpolation in the dying declaration (ii) contradiction in the statements of PW-11 and PW-16 regarding injuries on the palm, (iii) the victim with 80% injuries apparently not in a situation to talk or give statement, (iv) PW-2, son of the deceased himself stating that his mother committed suicide as she could not bear that her another son had been sent to jail, (v) there being no corroborative evidence to the statement and (vi) no other evidence led by the prosecution to connect the Appellants with the crime except the statement, he held it unsafe to convict the Appellants on the solitary basis of the dying declaration.

iii.   Appeals allowed. Impugned order of the High Court set aside.

CHAPTER FOUR

Mallappa Vs. State of Karnataka, 2021

Hon'ble Judges/Coram:

N.V. Ramana, C.J.I., Surya Kant and Aniruddha Bose, JJ.

Equivalent Citation: 2021(223)AIC113, 2021 (117) ACC 334, 2021 (2) ALT (Crl.) 191 (A.P.), 2021(3)BLJ444, 2021(2)Crimes273(SC), 2021(3)JKJ231[SC], 2021(4)KarLJ121, 2021(4)KCCR3171, 2021(2)MLJ(Crl)572, 2021(2)N.C.C.522, (2021)5SCC572, 2021 (4) SCJ 669, 2021(3)UC1441, MANU/SC/0345/2021

Relevant Section: Section 34 and 302 of the Indian Penal Code, 1860.

Number of Pages in the Original Judgment: 05

Case Note:

Criminal - Murder - Conviction - Sections 34, 302 of the Indian Penal Code, 1860 (IPC) - Appellant alongwith his son accused of murdering his brother - Trial Court acquitted Appellant - High Court in appeal set aside Trial Court's verdict and convicted Appellant - Hence, the present appeal - Whether High Court wrongly interfered with the finding of Trial Court?

Brief Facts:

The Appellant was charged with having committed murder of his brother. His sonwas the co-Accused. The Trial Court acquitted both of them from the charges. High Court in appeal set aside the decision of the Trial Court and Appellant of the offence punishable under Section 302 of the Code. It was alleged that there was previous dispute between the Appellant and the deceased victim over certain immovable properties and sharing of canal water, which were projected as the motive of the crime by the prosecution.The prosecution case was built up primarily on the evidence of witness presented as an eye-witness and witnesses who gave evidence as post occurrence witnesses.

Held, while allowing the Appeal:

i.   Witness does not inspire confidence.

ii.   The first Court of facts on appreciation of evidence had acquitted the Appellant. No major lacuna found in its reasoning which would have warranted interference by the Appeal Court for reversing such finding into that of guilt.

iii.   Impugned judgment set aside. The judgment of acquittal by the Trial Court sustained.

iv.   The appeal is allowed.

CHAPTER FIVE

The State of Odisha Vs. Banabihari Mohapatra and Ors., 2021

Hon'ble Judges/Coram:

Indira Banerjee and Hemant Gupta, JJ.

Equivalent Citation: 2021(220)AIC266, AIR2021SC1375, 2021 (2) ALD(Crl.) 198 (SC), 2021 (116) ACC 317, 2021ALLMR(Cri)1165, 132(2021)CLT305, 2021CriLJ2115, 2021(2)Crimes143(SC), 2021(1)JKJ339[SC], 2021(2)N.C.C.83, 2021(2)RCR(Criminal)187, 2021 (2) SCJ 607, MANU/SC/0101/2021

Relevant Section: Section 34, 302 and 201 of the Indian Penal Code, 1860.

Number of Pages in the Original Judgment: 07

Ratio Decidendi:

Suspicion, however strong cannot take the place of proof.

Case Note:

Criminal - Acquittal - Leave to appeal dismissed - Delay of 41 days - Offence committed punishable under Sections 302 and 201read with Section 34 of the Indian Penal Code, 1860 (IPC) - Petitionercontended High Court of committing gross error in dismissing leave to appeal on the ground of delay - Whether impugned finding sustainable and even otherwise on merits whether Respondent guilty of causing murder?

Brief Facts:

High Court vide impugned judgment dismissed State's application seeking leave to appeal against order of acquittal passed in favour of Accused/ Respondent. The Respondent was charged with Sections 302 and

201 read with Section 34 of the Indian Penal Code, 1860. Application for leave to appeal was rejected on the ground of delay, but after considering the merits of application for leave to appeal. As per Complainant, the deceased used to move around with the first Accused, who was having an electric sales and repairing shop. It was alleged that first Accused informed Complainant that the deceased had been lying motionless and still, not responding to calls. Deceased was seen lying dead inside a room which was locked, with a swollen belly and a deep burn injury on his right foot which was apparently caused by electric shock. The body of the deceased appeared black and blood was oozing out from the mouth and nostril of the deceased.The complainant alleged Accused No. 1, his son and other accomplices of murdering her husband by applying electric shock to him after administering some poisonous substances to him. Sessions Court held that prosecution had failed to prove the charges against the Accused Respondents.

Held, while dismissing the Special Leave Petition:

i.   The Prosecution miserably failed to establish the guilt of the Accused Respondents. The Trial Court rightly acquitted the Accused Respondents. There is no infirmity in the judgment of the Trial Court that calls for interference.

ii. Before a case against an Accused can be said to be fully established on circumstantial evidence, the circumstances from which the conclusion of guilt is to be drawn must fully be established and the facts so established should be consistent only with the hypothesis of guilt of the Accused. There has to be a chain of evidence so complete, as not to leave any reasonable doubt for any conclusion consistent with the innocence of the Accused and must show that in all human probability, the act must have been done by the Accused.

iii. Trial Court rightly acquitted the Accused Respondents. There is a strong possibility that the Accused, who was as per the opinion of the doctor who performed the autopsy, intoxicated with alcohol, might have accidentally touched a live electrical wire, may be while he was asleep. The impugned judgment of the High Court dismissing the appeal on the ground of delay does not call for interference under Article 136 of the Constitution of India.

iv. It is well settled by a plethora of judicial pronouncement of this Court that suspicion, however strong cannot take the place of proof. An

Accused is presumed to be innocent unless proved guilty beyond reasonable doubt.

v. No ground made out to interfere with the impugned judgment and order of the High Court. Consequently, the Special Leave Petition was dismissed.

CHAPTER SIX

Mihir Gope and Ors. Vs. The State of Jharkhand, 2021

Hon'ble Judges/Coram:

N.V. Ramana, Surya Kant and Aniruddha Bose, JJ.

Equivalent Citation: 2021(2)ACR1851, 2021(218)AIC15, AIR2021SC534, 2021 (1) ALD(Crl.) 912 (SC), 2021 (115) ACC 664, 2021 (2) ALT (Crl.) 96 (A.P.), 2021(1)BLJ240, 131(2021)CLT423, 2021CriLJ1110, 2021(1)Crimes22(SC), 2021(1)J.L.J.R.242, 2021(1)JKJ217[SC], 2021(1)N.C.C.354, 2021(1)PLJR331, (2021)2SCC726, 2021(1)UC47, MANU/SC/0010/2021

Relevant Section: Section 34, 302, 307, 325 and 341 of the Indian Penal Code, 1860.

Number of Pages in the Original Judgment: 08

Case Note:

Criminal - Acquittal - Lack of evidence - Sections 34, 302, 307, 325 and 341 of Indian Penal Code, 1860 - Two persons had died from injuries received in consequence of assaults on them over land related dispute - Appellants had been held guilty by Trial Court for committing offences under Sections 341, 307, 325, and 302 read with Section 34 of Code - On appeal, High Court confirmed judgment and order of conviction for alleged offences - Hence, present appeal - Whether prosecution prove its case beyond reasonable doubt.

Brief Facts:

The two persons had died from injuries received in consequence of assaults on them over a land related dispute. Certain other members of the Appellant's family were also injured on account of assault as a result of the same dispute. The cause of the dispute with the members of the deceased victims' family was specifically related to the construction of a hut. Appellants had been held guilty by the Trial Court for committing offences under Sections 341, 307, 325, and 302 read with Section 34 of the Indian Penal Code, 1860.

Held, while partly allowing the appeal:

i. It would be apparent from the evidence of the medical practitioners that there was only one injury on deceased's head whereas on other deceased's head, there was a probability that he suffered two injuries. But the injuries on deceased's head could not be said to have been caused by either axe or tangi, which were sharp edged weapons. Even if proceed on the basis that both axe and tangi had blunt sides and such blunt sides were used to strike, that very fact could not establish involvement of both accused in striking deceased persons. Thus, the Trial Court and the High Court had not rightly concluded on involvement of accused persons in assault of deceased persons so as to implicate them for murder under Section 302 read with Section 34 of the code. The eye witnesses' accounts, as we have already observed shows element of exaggeration and inconsistency in implicating both accused persons for their strikes on deceased. There was apparent inconsistency in the eye witness account in describing the assaults by these two Appellants on deceased persons. Prosecution witness had attributed assault on both deceased persons to father of Appellants and Appellants. This was a very generalised description. Prosecution witness had stated that accused persons had assaulted deceased. Thus, if compare the number of injuries on deceased as it transpires from the evidence of medical practitioners, which was three at the most, they did not match with the number of strikes made by accused persons, as stated on oath by these witnesses. This court could not rely on the account of assault given by these witnesses to the extent they relate to strikes by accused persons. This court consider it safer to rely on the evidence of prosecution witness, who had given specific and trustworthy account of the individual assaults. This court did not think the prosecution had been able to prove beyond reasonable doubt involvement of these two Appellants in delivering the blows to deceased persons.

ii. Though there were assaults by accused persons prosecution had failed to establish on the basis of evidence that these two Appellants shared common intention with their father. Their strikes on the victims can be segregated from those made by father of Appellants, as it transpires from evidence. Neither accused persons could be held to have been involved in assault on deceased, which forms the basis of conviction of the Appellants under Section 302 of the Code.

iii. However, there was sufficient evidence against accused persons of voluntarily causing hurt by the instruments. Both the Appellants guilty of committing offence under Section 324 of the Code.

CHAPTER SEVEN

Parvat Singh and Ors. Vs. State of Madhya Pradesh, 2020

Hon'ble Judges/Coram:

Ashok Bhushan and M.R. Shah, JJ.

Equivalent Citation: 2020(208)AIC1, 2020 (111) ACC 904, 2020 (2) ALT (Crl.) 1 (A.P.), 2021(3)BLJ454, 2020(1)Crimes405(SC), ILR[2020]MP1515, 2020(1)JCC664, 2020(2)JKJ358[SC], 2020(2)JLJ624, 2020(3)JLJ142, 2020(2)KLJ534, (2020)4SCC33, 2020 (5) SCJ 713, 2020(1)UC721, MANU/SC/0246/2020

Relevant Section: Section 149, 302 and 450 of the Indian Penal Code, 1860; Section 161 of Code of Criminal Procedure, 1973

Number of Pages in the Original Judgment: 07

Case Note:

Criminal - Acquittal - Sole eye witness - Sections 149, 302 and 450 of Indian Penal Code, 1860 and Section 161 of Code of Criminal Procedure, 1973 - Accused persons came to be tried by Trial Court for offences under Section 302 read with Section 149 of Code - Accused persons were charge-sheeted for offences punishable under Section 302 read with Section 149 and Section 450 of Code - After perusing evidence led by parties and solely relying upon the evidence of sole eye-witness, Trial Court convicted all Accused for offences under Section 302 read with Section 149 of Code - Feeling aggrieved, Appellants preferred appeal before High Court - High Court had dismissed appeal - Hence, present appeal - Whether sole eye witness was reliable and trustworthy witness to convict Appellants.

Brief Facts:

All the Accused persons came to be tried by the Learned Trial Court for the offences under Section 302 read with Section 149 of the Indian Penal Code. The Accused were charge-sheeted for the offences punishable under Section 302 read with Section 149 and Section 450 of the Indian Penal Code. The case was committed to the Court of Sessions. All the Accused pleaded not guilty, therefore, all the Accused came to be tried by the Learned Trial Court for the said offences. To prove the case against the Accused, the prosecution examined witnesses including informant - mother of the deceased who was the sole eyewitness. After perusing the evidence led by the parties and solely relying upon the evidence of the sole eye-witness, the Trial Court convicted all the Accused for the offences under Section 302 read with Section 149 of Indian Penal Code. Feeling aggrieved and dissatisfied with the judgment and order of conviction by the Trial Court, the Appellants herein-original Accused Nos. 2 to 5 preferred Criminal Appeal before the High Court. The High Court dismissed the appeal.

Held, while allowing the appeal:

i. It was required to be noted that it was a black night at the time of incident. The eye witness in her statement recorded under Section 161 Code of Criminal Procedure had stated that she had seen all the Accused in the light of the torch. She had stated that original Accused No. 1 was having an axe and other four were armed with lathis. She had also stated in her statement under Section 161 Code of Criminal Procedure that original Accused No. 1 gave the axe blow on the neck of the deceased due to the enmity and earlier dispute and other Accused were telling to run away immediately and thereafter all the five Accused ran away from behind the cattle shed/house. She stated that she had identified all the Accused in the light of the torch and also by voice. According to her after she shouted, other persons came. However, there was material improvement in her deposition before the Court. In her deposition, she had stated that Accused persons caught hold of deceased. In her deposition, she had also stated that there was a chimney light in the cattle shed. She had also stated in her deposition that the Accused ran away from the nearby agricultural field of sugarcane. Therefore, the deposition of eye witness was full of material contradictions and improvements so far as original Accused Nos. 2 to 5 was concerned. It was required to be noted that no other independent witness even named by eye witness had supported the case of the prosecution. Though, according to eye witness, she identified the Accused in the light of the torch, there was no recovery of torch. There was material improvement so far as the chimney light was concerned. In her deposition, she had not stated anything that the Appellants - original Accused Nos. 2 to 5 were having the lathis, though she had stated this in her statement under Section 161 Code of Criminal Procedure The High Court had observed relying upon her statement recorded under Section 161 Code of Criminal Procedure that the Appellants - Accused Nos. 2 to 5 were having lathis. Therefore, as such, the High Court had erred in relying upon the statement of eye witness recorded under Section 161 Code of Criminal Procedure while observing that the Appellants were having the lathis.

ii. In her statement under Section 161 Code of Criminal Procedure, eye witness had never stated that Accused persons caught hold of deceased, but stated that the Appellants told to run away as other persons have woken. In the facts and circumstances of the case, there were material contradictions, omissions and/or improvements so far as the Appellants - original Accused Nos. 2 to 5 were concerned and therefore it was not safe to convict the Appellants on the evidence of the sole witness of eye witness. The benefit of material contradictions, omissions and improvements must go in favour of the Appellants. Therefore, as such the Appellants were entitled to be given benefit of doubt.

Mohd. Akhtar and Ors. Vs. State of Bihar and Ors., 2018

Hon'ble Judges/Coram:

L. Nageswara Rao and R. Subhash Reddy, JJ.

Equivalent Citation: 2019(193)AIC17, 2019 (106) ACC 259, 2019(1)BLJ19, 2019(1)BomCR(Cri)491, 2018(4)Crimes482(SC), (2019)3GLR1921, 2019(1)J.L.J.R.184, 2019(2)JCC1236, 2019(1)N.C.C.102, 2019(1)PLJR260, 2018(15)SCALE432, (2019)2SCC513, 2019 (3) SCJ 365, 2018(3)UC2086, MANU/SC/1413/2018

Relevant Section: Section 34, 148 and 302 of the Indian Penal Code, 1860; Section 417 of Code of Criminal Procedure, 1973

Number of Pages in the Original Judgment: 06

Ratio Decidendi:

Presumption of innocence of Accused was further reinforced by acquittal order passed by trial Court.

Case Note:

Criminal - Conviction - Validity - Section 302, 34 and 148 of Indian Penal Code, 1860 (IPC) - In present Appeals, correctness of judgment of High Court by which judgment of trial court was set aside and acquittal of Appellants was reversed was questioned - High Court convicted Appellants under Section 302 read with Sections 34 and 148 of IPC and sentenced to undergo life imprisonment - Whether High Court was right in setting aside acquittal of Appellants and convicting m for an offence of murder.

Brief Facts:

In facts of present case, on completion of investigation, a charge sheet was filed Under Sections 148 and 302 read with Section 149 of IPC against seven persons out of whom one of Accused died and two absconded.

Remaining Accused i.e. Appellants-herein faced trial for charges framed under Sections 148 and 302 read with Section 149 of IPC. Trial court acquitted Appellants of all charges. However, High Court appreciated evidence and found fault with judgment of trial Court. High Court felt that apart from minor inconsistencies, evidence of eye witnesses was reliable and re was sufficient light to identify Accused. Delay in registering FIR was found to be not fatal to case of Prosecution. Evidence of interested witnesses was also held reliable by High Court. Minor errors in recording time in police station and non-examination of J.N. Singh (S.I.) did not prejudice prosecution's case. By differing with view taken by trial Court, High Court found that, judgment of trial Court was perverse and that was only one view possible which leads to guilt of Accused. High Court convicted Appellants under Section 302 read with Sections 34 and 148 of IPC and sentenced m to life imprisonment.

Held, while allowing the appeal:

i. Approach of High Court in an appeal against acquittals was explained in Surajpal Singh and Ors. v. State, It was well-established that, in an appeal under Section 417 of Code of Criminal Procedure, 1973 (CrPC), High Court had full power to review evidence upon which order of acquittal was founded, but it was equally well-settled that presumption of innocence of Accused was further reinforced by acquittal order passed by trial Court, and findings of trial court which had advantage of seeing witnesses and hearing their evidence could be reversed only for very substantial and compelling reasons.

ii. Interference with judgment of trial Court in case by High Court was on a re-appreciation of evidence which was undoubtedly permissible. Though High Court was aware of well-settled principles of law in matters relating to appeals against acquittals, it failed to apply same in their proper perspective. Interference with an order of acquittal was not permissible on ground that a different view was possible. If acquittal was justified on a probable view taken by trial Court, it should not be interfered with. Reasons given by trial Court for acquittal mainly pertain to delay in lodging FIR, untrustworthy eye witnesses, improbability of identification of Accused, non-examination of independent witnesses, previous enmity between Accused and witnesses, non-production of important prosecution witnesses and improper investigation of case. On a thorough examination of entire evidence on record and judgment of trial court, present Court was of view that, judgment of acquittal by trial Court was justified which ought not to have been interfered with by High Court. High Court brushed aside findings recorded by trial Court. High Court ignored fact that, presumption of innocence in favour of Appellants was further strengthened by an order of acquittal. No perversity in judgment of trial Court in acquitting Appellants had been demonstrated by High Court for interfering with judgment of trial court.

iii. Appeals allowed. Judgment of High Court was set aside and judgment of trial Court was restored.

CHAPTER NINE

Rama Kant Verma Vs. State of U.P. and Ors., 2008

Hon'ble Judges/Coram:

Dr. Arijit Pasayat, P. Sathasivam and Aftab Alam, JJ.

Equivalent Citation: 2009(74)AIC238, AIR2009SC1093, 2009 (64) ACC 714, I(2009)CCR81(SC), JT2008(13)SC84, 2008(16)SCALE233, (2008)17SCC257, MANU/SC/8343/2008

Relevant Section: Section 148, 149 and 302 of the Indian Penal Code, 1860; Article 136 of the Constitution

Number of Pages in the Original Judgment: 06

Ratio Decidendi:

"Courts can remit matters back to lower courts for fresh consideration, in interest of justice."

Case Note:

Criminal - Murder - Acquittal - Sections 302, 148 and 149 of Indian Penal Code, 1860 (IPC) - Present appeal is filed to challenge judgment and order of acquittal passed in a case for commission of offence punishable under Sections 302, 148 and 149 of IPC - Whether judgment and order of acquittal under challenge deserve interference - Held, in an appeal against acquittal, there is double presumption in favour of accused - Presumption of innocence is available to him - If accused has secured an order of acquittal, presumption of his innocence is re affirmed - It is strengthened by trial Court - If two reasonable conclusions are possible, Court should not disturb finding of acquittal - In present case, testimony of eye-witnesses, medical evidence and recoveries on record have been established beyond any doubt - There is no reason calling for non-interference with impugned order of acquittal - Judgment and order of acquittal is set aside - Appeal allowed.

Brief Facts:

An F.I.R. was lodged at 6.30 A.M. on 11.11.94 at Police Station, Tarun by Rama Kant (P.W. 1) with the allegation that his cousin Girish Varma was sleeping in the room of the Tube-well alongwith him. His grandfather Sukhai and his uncle Ram Naresh were sleeping under the Chhappar near the tube-well. His brother Umakant Varma (PW2) was sleeping inside the Saria for looking after the cattle. Sukhai and Ram Naresh raised alarm and asked for help, at which Ramakant alongwith Girish came out of the tube-well room after opening its door, and saw that Krishna Murari and Kashi Ram by means of Gandasa and Raghava Ram and Ram Milan by means of Banka, and 2-3 others, who had muffled/covered their faces by means of cloth were causing injuries to Sukhai and Ram Naresh. Ram Dev, another uncle of the informant, was sleeping south of the tube- well under the Chhappar. Ramakant, Umakant and Girish tried to rescue the victims, but the assailants attacked Girish and Ram Dev also by means of their weapons. Ramakant, Uma Kant escaped and ran into the field of Sugarcane and also raised alarm. It was night time 2.30 A.M. on 11 . 11.1994 (in between the night of 10th and 11th November, 1984). Due to cries and alarm raised by them, Ram Tej, father of informant, and several villagers came with lathis and torches. The assailants ran away towards south. It was further alleged that the four appellants were seen and identified by Ramakant (PW l) Uma Kant (PW 2), Ram Tej and villagers in the light of the torches and in the electricity light. It was also alleged that litigation in respect of land had been going on in between the victims and appellant Krishna Murari. The cattle of Krishna Murari were sent to the house of Ram Kripal ten days prior to the occurrence and he had also sent his family out of the village to his wife's house in another village. Rama Kant further alleged that in the morning Daljeet Singh (PW3), Jaising Mau and Hari Om (PW4) told him that on 10.11.94 at 9.00 A.M. the appellants were seen by them, taking non-vegetarian food alongwith Ram Tilak and Ram Kripal at the shop of Ram Kripal. Ramakant therefore, alleged his suspicion against Ram Kripal and Ram Tilak as the persons who were instrumental in the commission of this crime conspiring with the appellants. All the four victims had died on the spot. Leaving them there as such on the spot, he lodged the written report (Ext.Ka.1) at the Police Station where its check report (Ex.Ka.16) and G.D.entry(Ex.Ka.17) was prepared by Ram Harsh Yadava (PW 12) head constable and thus a case crime No. 156 of 94 was registered. Investigation was given to the Station Officer of the P.S. Sudhakar (PW 10) who, at the time of registering of the case, was busy in his duty at Ayodhya in "Chaulah

Kosi Parikarima" and who on receiving information of this case reached PS Tarun, and obtained copy of the FIR and other relevant papers from the PS and reached the spot of occurrence in village Bearauli at about 9.00 A.M. and found other police personnel including Riaz Khan of P.S, Haiderganj, and Sibte Haider SSI (PW13) of PS Tarun. He got the inquest reports of the dead Sukhai and Ram Naresh pre- pared through Riaz Khan. S.I. Riaz Khan died before the evidence and the inquest reports and connected papers Ext.Ka 25 to Ext.Ka 36 were proved by Ram Narain Pandey (PW 14) and also got the inquest reports in respect of deceased Ram Dev and Girish prepared through PW 13 Sibte Haider S.I. (Ex.Ka 17. 18 and Ka.20 to 24) under his supervision and direction. He sent the dead bodies for post mortem examination to Faizabad through con- stables at about 12.15 P.M. on that very day i.e. 11.11.1994.

Held, while allowing the appeal:

A doubt has been raised about the competence of a private party as distinguished from the State, to invoke the jurisdiction of this Court under Article 136 of the Constitution of India, 1950 (in short the 'Constitution') against a judgment of acquittal by the High Court. We do not see any substance in the doubt. Appellate power vested in this Court under Article 136 of the Constitution is not to be confused with ordinary appellate power exercised by appellate courts and appellate tribunals under specific statutes. It is a plenary power, 'exercisable outside the purview of ordinary law' to meet the pressing demands of justice See <u>Durga Shankar Mehta</u> v. <u>Thakur Raghuraj Singh</u> MANU/SC/0099/1954 : [1955]1SCR267 . Article 136 of the Constitution neither confers on anyone the right to invoke the jurisdiction of this Court nor inhibits anyone from invoking the Court's jurisdiction. The power is vested in this Court but the right to invoke the Court's jurisdiction is vested in no one. The exercise of the power of this Court is not circumscribed by any limitation as to who may invoke it. Where a judgment of acquittal by the High Court has led to a serious miscarriage of justice this Court cannot refrain from doing its duty and abstain from interfering on the ground that a private party and not the State has invoked the Court's jurisdiction. We do not have slightest doubt that we can entertain appeals against judgments of acquittal by the High Court at the instance of interested private parties also. The circumstance that the Criminal Procedure Code, 1973 (in short the "Code") does not provide for an appeal to the High Court against an order of acquittal by a subordinate Court, at the instance of a private party, has no relevance to the question of the power of this Court under Article 136. We may mention that in <u>Mohan Lal</u> v. <u>Ajit Singh</u> MANU/SC/0127/1978 : 1978CriLJ1107 this Court interfered with a judgment of acquittal by the High Court at the instance of a private party. An apprehension was expressed that if appeals against judgments of acquittal at the instance of private parties are permitted there may be a flood of appeals. We do not share the apprehension. Appeals under Article 136 of the Constitution are entertained by special leave granted by this Court, whether it is the State or a private party that invokes the jurisdiction of this Court, and special leave is not granted as a matter of course but only for good and sufficient reasons, well established by the practice of this Court.

In the circumstances, we deem it proper to remit the matter to the High Court for hearing the cases afresh and dispose them of in accordance with law. The appeals are allowed.

CHAPTER TEN

Pulicherla Nagaraju Vs. State of Andhra Pradesh, 2006

Hon'ble Judges/Coram:

G.P. Mathur and R.V. Raveendran, JJ.

Equivalent Citation: 2006(3)ACR2826(SC), 2006(46)AIC382, AIR2006SC3010, AIR2006SC3010, 2006 (Suppl.) ACC 195, 2006(3)ALT(Cri)232, 2006((3))ALT(Cri)232, III(2006)CCR274(SC), 2006CriLJ3899, 2006(3)Crimes233(SC), 2006-2-LW(Crl)833, 2006(4)RCR(Criminal)95, RLW2007(1)SC419, 2006(8)SCALE133, (2006)11SCC444, [2006]Supp(4)SCR633, MANU/SC/8419/2006

Relevant Section: Section 302 of the Indian Penal Code, 1860.

Number of Pages in the Original Judgment: 10

Case Note:

i. Indian Penal Code, 1860 - Section 302--Murder--Acquittal by trial court--But conviction and sentence by High Court--Whether justified?--Held, "yes"--P.Ws. 1 and 2 being related witnesses and inimically disposed towards accused--Nothing in their cross-examination to discredit their evidence--Their testimony finding corroboration from other evidence on record--Absence of any other injury except dagger injury caused by accused appellant--Is consistent with allegations in complaint--Deceased unarmed--Facts showing that intention of appellant was to cause death or at all events, cause bodily injury sufficient in ordinary course of nature to cause death--No merit in contention that whenever death is on account of single blow, offence is one under Section 304 and not Section 302--Intention to cause death--How can be gathered--Appellant carrying dangerous weapon--Previous enmity --In earlier incident, father and brother of deceased attacked

by appellant and his father--No provocation, sudden quarrel or fight--
No indication of any cause of apprehension of attack on appellant by
deceased--Stabbing was with great force causing injury on vital part
of body sufficient in ordinary course of nature to cause death--
Circumstances to bring case under Exception 4 to Section 300 not
existing--No reason to interfere.

ii. It is well-settled that evidence of a witness cannot be discarded merely
on the ground that he is either partisan or interested or closely related
to the deceased, if it is otherwise found to be trustworthy and credible.
It only requires scrutiny with more care and caution, so that neither
the guilty escape nor the innocent wrongly convicted. If on such careful
scrutiny, the evidence is found to be reliable and probable, it can be acted
upon. If it is found to be improbable or suspicious, it ought to be rejected.
Where the witness has a motive to falsely implicate the accused, his
testimony should have corroboration in regard to material particulars
before it is accepted.

iii. It is for the Courts to ensure that the cases of murder punishable under
Section 302, I.P.C. are not converted into offences punishable under
Section 304 Part I/II, or cases of culpable homicide not amounting
to murder, are treated as murder punishable under Section 302. The
intention to cause death can be gathered generally from a combination of
a few or several of the following, among other, circumstances : (i) nature
of the weapon used ; (ii) whether the weapon was carried by the accused
or was picked up from the spot ; (iii) whether the blow is aimed at a vital
part of the body ; (iv) the amount of force employed in causing injury
; (v) whether the act was in the course of sudden quarrel or sudden
fight or free for all fight ; (vi) whether the incident occurs by chance
or whether there was any pre-meditation ; (vii) whether there was any
prior enmity or whether the deceased was a stranger ; (viii) whether
there was any grave and sudden provocation, and if so, the cause for such
provocation ; (ix) whether it was in the heat of passion ; (x) whether
the person inflicting the injury has taken undue advantage or has acted
in a cruel and unusual manner ; (xi) whether the accused dealt a single
blow or several blows. The above list of circumstances is, of course, not
exhaustive and there may be several other special circumstances with
reference to individual cases which may throw light on the question of
intention.

iv. Code of Criminal Procedure, 1973--Sections 378 (2), 385 and 386--Appeal against acquittal--Power of High Court not different from appeal against conviction--Factors for consideration by High Court.

v. It is now well settled that the power of the High Court in an appeal from acquittal is no different from its power in an appeal from conviction. It can review and consider the entire evidence and come to its own conclusions by either accepting the evidence rejected by the trial court or rejecting the evidence accepted by the trial court. However, if the High Court decided to depart from the conclusions reached by the trial court, it should pay due attention to the grounds on which acquittal was based and state the reasons as to why it finds the conclusions leading to the acquittal, unacceptable. It should also bear in mind that (i) the presumption of innocence in favour of the accused is fortified by the findings of the trial court ; (ii) the accused is entitled to benefit of any doubt ; and (iii) the trial court had the advantage of examining the demeanour of the witnesses. The crux of the matter, however, is whether the High Court is able to give clear reasons to dispel the doubt raised, and reject the reasons given by the trial court.

Brief Facts:

i. P. Narasimha Reddy (PW-2) and P. Govinda Reddy (Accused No. 1) are brothers. P. Dilli Babu Reddy (PW-1) and Purushotham Reddy (deceased) are the sons of Narasimha Reddy. Ranamma (Accused No. 2) is the wife of Govinda Reddy. Nagaraja Reddy (Accused No. 3), Balakrishna Reddy @ 'Balu' and Chandrababu Reddy @ 'Babu' are the sons of Govinda Reddy and Ranamma. (Balu and Babu were juveniles at the relevant time). Both families were residents of Bangareddipalli Diguva Indlu, a hamlet falling under the Gangadhara Nellore Panchayat in Chittoor District. The house of Narasimha Reddy and house of Govinda Reddy were separated by the land of Chinnakka.

ii. Narasimha Reddy, after his marriage, having differences with his parents had shifted to his father-in-law's place and then to Madras. Ultimately, he came back to his native village. In the meanwhile, Govinda Reddy and two other brothers namely Krishna Reddy and Venkateswarulu Reddy had continued to live with their father Bakki Reddy. Bakki Reddy and Venkateswarulu Reddy had died and Krishna Reddy was residing in a different town. Govinda Reddy was in possession and enjoyment of the family properties. There were disputes between the families of Narasimha Reddy and Govinda Reddy in regard to property.

iii. On 24.4.1999, Narasimha Reddy (PW-2) brought some plastic pipes to his house in a hired tractor. Accused 1, 2 and 3 (Govinda Reddy, his wife and son Nagaraja Reddy) came to the house of Narasimha Reddy and raised a quarrel stating that the tractor unauthorizedly passed through their land and threatened Narasimha Reddy with dire consequences. This was the first incident.

iv. On 25.4.1999 at about 6 p.m., Govinda Reddy with his wife (A2) and sons (A3 and two juveniles) removed a part of the fence surrounding Narasimha Reddy's property. When Narasimha Reddy and his son Dilli Babu Reddy rushed to the place and questioned why they were removing the fence, Accused 1, 2 and 3 started abusing them. Govinda Reddy (A1) exhorted his wife and sons to kill Narasimha Reddy and Dilli Babu Reddy. Nagaraja Reddy (A-3) dealt a blow on the right side of Dilli Babu Reddy's head with the upper side of a 'Barisa' (a long dagger with a long handle). Then, Govinda Reddy (A1) dealt a blow on the right middle finger of Narasimha Reddy with a sickle. Both Narasimha and Dilli Babu Reddy sustained bleeding injuries. The neighbouring land owners and others working in the adjoining fields rushed and separated the two groups. This was the second incident.

v. Within about half an hour of the second incident, Purushotham Reddy (first son of Narasimha Reddy) returned home. Narasimha Reddy and Dilli Babu Reddy narrated to him what had happened. Immediately, Purushotham Reddy, followed by his father (PW-2) and brother (PW-1), went towards the house of Govinda Reddy to question them about their high-handed acts. When Purushotham Reddy entered the land Chinnaka which was situated between the lands (houses) of the two brothers, accused 1, 2, & 3 (Govinda Reddy, Ranamma and Nagaraja Reddy) along with two juvenile sons of Accused No. 1 (Balu and Babu) came from their house. Govinda Reddy was armed with a stick with nails, Ranamma was armed with stout stick, Nagaraja was armed with a Barisa. Govinda Reddy exhorted his wife and sons to kill Purushotham Reddy. Balu and Babu threw mud balls at Narasimha Reddy and Dilli Babu Reddy, who were following Purushotham Reddy. Govinda Reddy and Ranamma caught hold of Purushotham Reddy and Nagaraja (A-3) stabbed Purushotham Reddy near his throat with the Barisa. Purushotham Reddy collapsed. Govinda Reddy and his wife and children ran away. This was the third incident. It occurred around 7.30 P.M. This incident was witnessed by Gurava Reddy (PW-3), Gungulu Reddy (PW-4), Perumal's son Dilli Babu (PW-5) and P. Ravi (PW-6) and Sarojamma. But they did not interfere.

vi. Thereafter, Dilli Babu Reddy (PW-1) got a complaint (Ex.P-1) written and presented it at the Gangadhara Nellore Police Station (which was at a distance of about 4 km. from the place of incident) around 9.00 P.M. The police sent Narasimha Reddy and Dilli Babu Reddy for treatment to Primary Health center for examination and treatment.

Held, while acquitting the accused:

i. In this case, as noticed above, the appellant was carrying a Barisa, a dangerous weapon. There was previous enmity. There was an earlier incident, about half an hour earlier when the father and brother of the deceased had been attacked by the appellant and his father. The deceased was unarmed. There was no provocation, sudden quarrel or fight. There was no indication of any cause for an apprehension on the part of the appellant that the deceased may attack him. The stabbing was with great force, causing an injury on a vital part of body, sufficient in the ordinary course of nature to cause death. The description of the injury and cause for death given by PW-11, who conducted the post mortem is telling:

ii. An incised injury 5 cm x 3 cm x 12 cm deep over right supra clavicle fossa above the medial end of right clavicle... sub-clavier artery is severed....An incised injury 4cm x 1cm x 2cm deep over the apex of right lung ...deceased would appear to have died due to haemorrhage and shock due to injuries to right sub-clavier artery and upper lobe of right lung.

iii. The intention to cause death or at all events intention of causing bodily injury which is sufficient in the ordinary course of nature to cause death was made out. The circumstances to bring the case under Exception (4) to Section 300 do not exist.

iv. We accordingly find no reason to interfere with the decision of the High Court convicting the appellant. The appeal is dismissed.

CHAPTER ELEVEN

Manoj Kumar Khokhar Vs. State of Rajasthan and Ors., 2022

Hon'ble Judges/Coram:

M.R. Shah and B.V. Nagarathna, JJ.

Equivalent Citation: AIR2022SC364, 2022(1)CTC817, MANU/SC/0028/2022

Relevant Section: Section 302 of the Indian Penal Code, 1860

Number of Pages in the Original Judgment: 11

Case Note:

Criminal - Bail - Appeal against grant thereof - FIR alleged commission of offence under Section 302 of the Indian Penal Code, 1860 (IPC) - Pre-existing rivalry between Accused, his brothers and deceased - Accused enlarged on Bail - Hence the present appeal - Whether bail granted liable to be set aside?

Brief Facts:

Appellant is the son of deceased and one who lodged the First Information Report for alleged offence under Section 302 IPC against R2/Accused. As alleged in the FIR lodged by Appellant, he was attacked by the Respondent-Accusedwith the intention of killing him. Respondent-Accused pinned the deceased to the ground, sat on his chest and forcefully strangled him, thereby causing his death. As stated in the FIR, there was a pre-existing rivalry between the Respondent-Accused, his brothers and the deceased.The Respondent-Accused was arrested and remained under judicial custody for nearly one year and five months till granted bail by the High Court vide impugned order.

Held, while allowing the Appeal:

i. Court considering an application for bail has to exercise discretion in a judicious manner and in accordance with the settled principles of law having regard to the crime alleged to be committed by the Accused on the one hand and ensuring purity of the trial of the case on the other.

ii. While elaborate reasons may not be assigned for grant of bail or an extensive discussion of the merits of the case may not be undertaken by the court considering a bail application, an order de hors reasoning or bereft of the relevant reasons cannot result in grant of bail.

iii. Having considered facts of the present case, case not considered fit for grant of bail to the Respondent-Accused, having regard to the seriousness of the allegations against him.

iv. High Court has lost sight of the aforesaid material aspects of the case and has, by a very cryptic and casual order, de hors coherent reasoning, granted bail to the Accused. Hence the impugned order set aside. The appeal is allowed.

CHAPTER TWELVE

Brijmani Devi Vs. Pappu Kumar and Ors., 2021

Hon'ble Judges/Coram:

L. Nageswara Rao, B.R. Gavai and B.V. Nagarathna, JJ.

Equivalent Citation: 2022(2)BLJ114, 2022(1)JLJ120, 2022(1)RCR(Criminal)515, MANU/SC/1274/2021

Relevant Section: Section 302 r/w 34 of the Indian Penal Code, 1860; Section 27 of the Arms Act, 1959

Number of Pages in the Original Judgment: 10

Case Note:

Criminal - Bail - Offences allegedly committed under Section 302 read with Section 34 of the Indian Penal Code, 1860 (IPC) and Section 27 of the Arms Act, 1959 - Sessions Court rejected bail application considering past antecedents as well - High Court however granted bail vide impugned judgment - Hence, the present appeal - Whether High Court erred in granting bail considering that Respondent Accused was already involved in other crimes and a habitual offender?

Brief Facts:

The present appeals were preferred by the informant (mother of deceased son) assailing the orders passed by High Court granting bail to the Accused, a common Respondent in the appeals.Appellant, the mother of deceased, stated to be an eyewitness to the killing of her son and also the person who lodged the First Information Report for offence of murder of her son. Appellant contended that High Court erred in granting bail without considering Accused's involvement in previous several FIRs and also a habitual offender. Hence, the present appeal.

Held, while allowing the Appeal:

i. While liberty of an individual is an invaluable right, at the same time while considering an application for bail Courts cannot lose sight of the serious nature of the accusations against an Accused and the facts that have a bearing in the case, particularly, when the accusations may not be false, frivolous or vexatious in nature but are supported by adequate material brought on record so as to enable a Court to arrive at a prima facie conclusion.

ii. Court considering an application for bail has to exercise discretion in a judicious manner and in accordance with the settled principles of law having regard to the crime alleged to be committed by the Accused on the one hand and ensuring purity of the trial of the case on the other.

iii. While elaborating reasons may not be assigned for grant of bail, at the same time an order de hors reasoning or bereft of the relevant reasons cannot result in grant of bail. It would be only a non speaking order which is an instance of violation of principles of natural justice. In such a case the prosecution or the informant has a right to assail the order before a higher forum.

iv. The High court has lost sight of vital aspects of the case and in very cryptic orders granted bail to the Respondent-Accused. High Court was not right in allowing the applications for bail filed by the Respondent-Accused. Hence, the impugned orders passed by the High Court are set aside. The appeals are allowed.

CHAPTER THIRTEEN

Saranya Vs. Bharathi and Ors., 2021

Hon'ble Judges/Coram:

Dr. D.Y. Chandrachud and M.R. Shah, JJ.

Equivalent Citation: 2021(225)AIC91, AIR2021SC3948, 2021 (117) ACC 653, 2021 (3) ALT (Crl.) 225 (A.P.), 2021(5)BLJ236, 2021CriLJ4150, 2021(3)Crimes292(SC), 2021(4)JKJ19[SC], 2021(3)MLJ(Crl)640, 2021(3)N.C.C.413, 2021(4)RCR(Criminal)46, 2021(4)RLW2959(SC), (2021)8SCC583, 2021(3)UC1803, MANU/SC/0547/2021

Relevant Section: Section 482 of the Code of Criminal Procedure, 1973; Sections 34, 326, 307, 302, 420 of the Indian Penal Code, 1860

Number of Pages in the Original Judgment: 07

Case Note:

Criminal - Quashing of FIR - Section 482 of the Code of Criminal Procedure, 1973 (CrPC) - FIR registered under Sections 326, 307, 302, 420 read with Section 34 of the Indian Penal Code, 1860 (IPC) - High Court vide impugned judgment quashed and set aside entire proceedings qua R1/ Original Accused No. 2(A2) - Present appeal by original Complainant-Wife of the deceased-victim - Whether High Court erred in quashing the proceedings vide impugned judgment?

Brief Facts:

FIR in the instant matter came to be registered at the instance of wife of the deceased. The deceased had lost his job. He subsequently came into contact with R1 who assured him to arrange job against money. Deceased paid substantial amount however nothing happened even after six months. When pursued, R1 called deceased and Appellant for a meeting and offered 'Prasadam' from ShirdiSai Baba Temple. After consuming, Appellant's husband died. Complainant wife fainted and got her statement recorded in hospital in form of dying declaration though eventually she survived. Hence, her statement could not be assumed as dying declaration. The instant appeal was against High Court's order directing quashing of proceedings. Hence, the present appeal.

Held, while allowing the Appeal:

i. In the present case, there is sufficient material on record raising the strong suspicion against Respondent No. 1 herein-A2 also.

ii. During the course of the investigation, the investigating officer has collected very important evidence in the form of call details between A1 & A2 which are in the proximity of the time of commission of offence and even thereafter. Therefore, in the facts and circumstances of the case, when Respondent No. 1 herein has been chargesheeted for the offences under Sections 420, 302 r/w 109 Indian Penal Code and as observed hereinabove when there is ample material to show at least a prima facie case against Respondent No. 1 herein-A2, the High Court has committed a grave error in quashing the chargesheet/entire criminal proceedings qua her in exercise of powers under Section 482 Code of Criminal Procedure. Quashing the chargesheet against the Accused is not justified.

iii. Impugned judgment and order passed by the High Court quashing the chargesheet/criminal proceedings in quashed and set aside. Appeal allowed.

CHAPTER FOURTEEN

Guru Dutt Pathak Vs. State of Uttar Pradesh, 2021

Hon'ble Judges/Coram:

Dr. D.Y. Chandrachud and M.R. Shah, JJ.

Equivalent Citation: 2021(3)ACR2553, 2021(4)ADJ643, 2021(223)AIC81, AIR2021SC2257, 2021 (2) ALD(Crl.) 623 (SC), 2021(4) ALJ 487, 2021 (117) ACC 309, 2021 (3) ALT (Crl.) 232 (A.P.), 2021CriLJ3281, 2021(2)Crimes232(SC), 2021(3)JKJ118[SC], 2021(2)N.C.C.481, (2021)6SCC116, 2021 (4) SCJ 602, MANU/SC/0342/2021

Relevant Section: Sections 34, 302 or 302 of the Indian Penal Code, 1860

Number of Pages in the Original Judgment: 14

Case Note:

Criminal - Conviction - Offence committed under Sections 34, 302 of the Indian Penal Code, 1860 (IPC) - High Court vide impugned judgment set aside Trial Court's judgment acquitting Appellant - Hence, the present appeal - Whether in the facts and circumstances of the case, High Court was justified in interfering with the order of acquittal passed by the learned trial Court?

Brief Facts:

Appellant/ Accused No. 4 is in appeal against High Court's impugned judgment reversing order of acquittal passed by the trial Court acquitting Accused for the offences punishable under Sections 34, 302 of the Indian Penal Code. It was alleged by prosecution that deceased was the Pradhan of village and Accused were having grudge against him. The deceased was allegedly attacked by the Accused with spear and lathis. Trial Court acquitted all the Accused persons mainly on the grounds that eyewitnesses were related and interested witnesses and no independent witness was examined. Sons of the deceased were termed as chance witnesses and place of occurrence was not proved. High Court however reversed the finding of Trial Court to convict Appellant. Hence, the present appeal.

Held, while dismissing the Appeal:

Considering the facts and circumstances of the case and on re-appreciation of the evidence, when the High Court has come to the conclusion that the findings recorded by the learned trial Court while acquitting the Accused were perverse and even contrary to the evidence on record and/or misreading of the evidence, the High Court rightly interfered with the judgment and order of acquittal passed by the learned trial Court and has rightly convicted the Accused. In the present case, the Appellant was specifically named right from the very beginning in the FIR. He has been attributed the specific role. The same has been established and proved from the evidence of PW4. No error has been committed by the High Court in interfering with the judgment and order of acquittal passed by the learned trial Court.

No reason to interfere with the impugned judgment and order passed by the High Court reversing the acquittal and convicting the Accused.The present appeal is accordingly dismissed.

CHAPTER FIFTEEN

State of Rajasthan and Ors. Vs. Bablu and Ors., 2021

Hon'ble Judges/Coram:

U.U. Lalit and Ajay Rastogi, JJ.

Equivalent Citation: 2022(1)RCR(Criminal)189, MANU/SC/1134/2021

Relevant Section: Sections 147, 148, 149, 450 or 450/149, 452 or 452/149, 302 or 302 read with Sections 149, 307 or 307 read with 149 of the Indian Penal Code, 1860

Number of Pages in the Original Judgment: 12

Case Note:

Criminal - Appeal against Acquittal - FIR registered alleged offences under Sections 147, 148, 149, 450 or 450/149, 452 or 452/149, 302 or 302 read with Sections 149, 307 or 307 read with 149 of the Indian Penal Code, 1860 (IPC) - Trial Court convicted all Accused - In appeal eleven out of thirteen accused acquitted - State in appeal challenging acquittal - Convicted accused challenged conviction for want of proper evidence - Whether impugned judgment liable to be set aside or sustainable?

Brief Facts:

The present appeals were preferred by the State and original informant challenging the acquittal of eleven Accused persons out of total thirteen persons. Two were convicted. An FIR came to be registered on a written report made by complainant alleging entering into complainant's house and attacking victims. Trial Court convicted all the Accused persons. High Court in appeal affirmed conviction of A2 and A3 while acquitting others. Hence the present appeal.

Held, while partly allowing the Appeals:

i. Even the version of a single witness, if his testimony is found reliable by the Court, can be the foundation of the order of conviction.In the instant case, the evidence of PW1, the brother of the deceased itself would normally be sufficient.

ii. In the face of clear, consistent and cogent evidence on record, the High Court was not justified in proceeding on the basis that the eyewitnesses had not named other Accusedin specific terms or entertaining any doubt and then recording order of acquittal. The approach of the High Court was completely against the settled principles of law and no valid reasons were given by the High Court as to why the evidence of all the eyewitnesses could not be relied upon in so far as the role played by the acquitted Accused was concerned. The order of acquittal recorded by the High Court to be completely unjust and its conclusion to be totally against the record.

iii. Considering the entirety of the material on record, what emerges is the consistent and cogent eyewitness account on record through PWs 1 and 27, which was well supported by PWs 2, 24 and 25.

iv. In the circumstances, appeals allowed against original Accused A1, A6, A7, A8, A10 and A13 while rest of the Accused-Respondents are given benefit of doubt and their acquittal, as recorded by the High Court is confirmed. The order of conviction and sentence recorded against original Accused A1, A6, A7, A8, A10 and A13 by the Trial Court is thus restored. These appeals are partly allowed to the extent indicated.

CHAPTER SIXTEEN

Indrapal Singh and Ors. Vs. State of U.P., 2021

Hon'ble Judges/Coram:

L. Nageswara Rao, B.R. Gavai and B.V. Nagarathna, JJ.

Equivalent Citation: 2021(10)ADJ315, 2021(227)AIC56, AIR2021SC4514, 2022 (118) ACC 264, 2021(4)Crimes110(SC), 2021(5)JKJ298[SC], 2021(4)RCR(Criminal)225, MANU/SC/0682/2021

Relevant Section: Sections 34, 302 of the Indian Penal Code, 1860

Number of Pages in the Original Judgment: 08

Case Note:

Criminal - Conviction - Sections 34, 302 of the Indian Penal Code, 1860 (IPC) - Appellants contended inconsistency on testimonies of eye-witness - Besides, post mortem reports stated to be without FIR numbers mentioned on them - Whether conviction as directed in the given circumstances sustainable?

Brief Facts:

The present appeals were filed by the Appellants aggrieved by the dismissal of their appeals challenging conviction. The Trial Court on the basis of oral evidence and material on record convicted and sentenced the Appellants. Trial court found charges leveled against them duly proved by the prosecution. High Court confirmed the findings of Trial Court and hence the present appeal.

Held, while dismissing the Appeal:

i. The deposition of PW1 and PW2 consistent and coherent. They have withstood the cross-examination of the defence and nothing contrary or incriminating found.

ii. No substance in the contention of the learned Counsel for the Appellants-Accused that there was an attempt to improve the case of the prosecution than what had been actually mentioned in the complaint Exb. ka1 and the FIR Exb. Ka-34.

iii. In fact, a cumulative reading of the evidence of PW1 and PW2 along with other material evidence on record would clearly point to the fact that Section 34 of the Indian Penal Code was rightly invoked along with Section 302 vis-o?=-vis the Accused. Contention raised by the learned Counsel for the Accused-Appellants is without substance and in fact, it is contrary to the evidence on record.

iv. There is no explanation by the defence as to why all the four assailants came together. The incident occurred in broad-day light and the complaint given by PW1 within two hours of the incident could not be an exact narration of the incident with minute details, but the FIR contained ingredients so as to register an FIR under Section 302 and Section 302 read with Section 34 against all the Accused.

v. No merit in theappeals. Conviction upheld. Appeals dismissed.

CHAPTER SEVENTEEN

Lala Vs. The State of Maharashtra, 2021

Hon'ble Judges/Coram:

Sanjay Kishan Kaul and Hrishikesh Roy, JJ.

Equivalent Citation: 2021(3)ACR2849, 2021(225)AIC85, AIR2021SC5199, 2021 (117) ACC 622, 2021ALLMR(Cri)3482, 2021(5)BLJ382, 2021(3)Crimes254(SC), 2021(4)JKJ11[SC], 2021(3)N.C.C.431, 2021(4)RCR(Criminal)41, MANU/SC/0548/2021

Relevant Section: Sections 120B, 147, 148, 302 and 324 of the Indian Penal Code, 1860

Number of Pages in the Original Judgment: 06

Case Note:

Criminal - Conviction - Sections 120B, 147, 148, 302 and 324 of the Indian Penal Code, 1860 (IPC) - Judgment directing conviction assailed on the grounds of Appellant's identity not established - Further prosecution also failed to conduct test identification parade (TIP) to establish Appellant's identity - Whether in such circumstances, order of conviction as directed liable to be interfered with?

Brief Facts:

The present appeal was filed against judgment directing conviction. It was submitted by Appellant and the injured informant did not take his name while naming others in the FIR registered. Findings of Courts below based on ocular evidence of 4 eyewitnesses. Appellant argued to be not amongst the six named and other Accused in the FIR. Moreover, the prosecution also did not arrange for a Test Identification Parade (TIP) and thus Appellant's not clearly established.

Held, while dismissing the Appeals:

TIP was unnecessary in the present case as the identity of the Appellant was known to the witnesses and he was specifically identified by PW1, and PW2 as the person who wielded the sword and inflicted the injuries.

Identity of the Appellant as one of the attacking group members and his specific role in the assault is established beyond doubt. The prosecution produced cogent evidence of the Appellant being part of a conspiracy by all the Accused in the assault which led to the death of deceased and injuries to PW1 and others. As such, the conviction of the Appellant by the trial court, as upheld by the High Court, cannot be faulted.

No grounds to interfere with the impugned judgment.

CHAPTER EIGHTEEN

Rajendra Singh Vs. State of Uttaranchal, 2013

Hon'ble Judges/Coram:

Aftab Alam and Ranjana Prakash Desai, JJ.

Equivalent Citation: 2013(3)ACR2811, 2013V AD (S.C.) 21, 2013(126)AIC217, 2013(3)AJR436, 2013(4) ALJ 378, 2013ALLMR(Cri)1870, 2013ALLMR(Cri)1870(SC), II(2013)CCR262(SC), 2013CriLJ3172, 2013(2)Crimes194(SC), JT2013(7)SC438, 2013(5)SCALE568, (2013)4SCC713, [2013]2SCR783, MANU/SC/0359/2013

Relevant Section: Sections 302 of the Indian Penal Code, 1860

Number of Pages in the Original Judgment: 07

Ratio Decidendi:

"Order of conviction shall be passed when there is sufficient evidence to prove guilt of Accused."

Case Note:

Indian Penal Code, 1860 - Section 302--Murder--Acquittal by trial court--Conviction and sentence by High Court--Validity--Deceased was killed by inflicting injuries by pair of scissors--Trial court acquitted appellant on basis of discrepancies in depositions of eye-witnesses--Medical evidence consistent with prosecution case--P.W. 2 and P.W. 3 fully supported prosecution case in regard to assault by appellant on deceased with pair of scissors--P.W. 3 (wife of deceased) deposed before court regarding genesis of occurrence--Deposition of P.W. 3 in regard to assault by appellant or deceased--Quite graphic--Appellant picked up blood stained scissors from shop counter and produced it before Investigating Officer--High Court rightly rejected view taken by trial court and rightly accepted evidences of P.W. 2 and P.W. 3 in order to bring home guilt of appellant--

Conviction and sentence awarded by High Court--Upheld.

Brief Facts:

i. This appeal is directed against the judgment and order dated April 30, 2008 passed by the Uttarakhand High Court in Government Appeal No. 1174 of 2001 (Old No. 303 of 1991). By the impugned judgment, the High Court allowed the Government Appeal, set aside the judgment of acquittal rendered by the trial court, and finding the Appellant guilty of the offence of murder convicted him Under Section 302 of the Penal Code and gave him the sentence of rigorous imprisonment for life.

ii. The case of the prosecution is based on a written report dated July 26, 1988 submitted at Police Station Dehradun by one Vijay Singh s/o. Puran Singh Rana (hereinafter referred to as "the informant"). In the written report it was stated that the informant's elder brother, namely, Kishan Singh Rana (the deceased) was a peon in the Bank of India, Rajpur Road Branch, Dehradun. He had given a pair of pants and some cloth for stitching to Rajendra Singh tailor (the Appellant), whose shop is on the road just near their house. The Appellant did not return the stitched clothes even after several days and on the evening prior to the date of occurrence, there was a quarrel between the informant's brother and the Appellant on that issue. On July 26, 1988 (the date of occurrence) the informant's brother had gone to the bank as usual on his motor cycle. He returned from the bank at about 1:00 p.m. and as he reached in front of the Appellant's shop, he got down from the motor cycle as the road was broken at that point. At that instant, the Appellant came out of his shop carrying a pair of scissors in his hands; hurling abuses, he came down to the road and attacked the informant's brother with the scissors with the intent to kill him. In order to save his life, Kishan Singh Rana ran down the road but the Appellant chased him and caught him after some distance in front of Chintamani's house. At that spot he gave the informant's brother many blows by the scissors, one after the other. Kishan Singh Rana fell down bleeding on the road. It was further stated in the written report that besides the informant, Makhan Singh (PW. 2), Laxman (Motor) Auto Mechanic (not examined) and his sister-in-law, Deepa (the wife of the deceased - PW. 3) and many other persons and women of the area witnessed the occurrence. After assaulting the deceased, the Appellant fled away from there. It was further stated in the written report that Makhan Singh took the informant's brother to

Dun Hospital, where he was declared brought dead. The written report concluded with the request to take legal action against the Appellant.

iii. The written report submitted by Vijay Singh was incorporated in the first information report (report No. 230) giving rise to criminal case No. 483/88/- Under Section 302 Indian Penal Code, P.S. Dehradun.

Held, while dismissing the appeal:

i. On a careful consideration of the materials on record and the submissions made on behalf of the Appellant and the State, we are of the view that the High Court has rightly rejected the view taken by the trial court as wholly untenable and has rightly accepted the evidences of PW. 2 and PW. 3 in order to bring home the guilt of the Appellant.

ii. In the light of the discussion above, we find no merit in the appeal. It is, accordingly, dismissed.

iii. The bail bonds of the Appellant are cancelled and he is directed to surrender within four weeks from today, failing which the trial court is directed to take all possible measures to apprehend him to make him undergo the remaining sentence.

CHAPTER NINETEEN

The State of Andhra Pradesh Vs. M. Narasimha Rao, 2010

Hon'ble Judges/Coram:

H.S. Bedi and C.K. Prasad, JJ.

Equivalent Citation: AIR2010SC3776, 2011(1)ALD(Cri)388, 2011 (72) ACC 541, 2010(4)BLJ44, IV(2010)CCR96(SC), 2010(2)CLJ(SC)325, [2011(1)JCR272(SC)], JT2010(9)SC235, 2011(1)RCR(Criminal)536, 2010(8)SCALE617, (2010)9SCC166, [2010]10SCR533, 2010(3)UC1385, MANU/SC/0650/2010

Relevant Section: Sections 302 of the Indian Penal Code, 1860

Number of Pages in the Original Judgment: 05

Ratio Decidendi:

"Unimpeachable evidence of late delivery of special report will do no great damage to prosecution story."

Case Note:

Indian Penal Code, 1860--Section 302--Murder--Acquittal--Legality-- Appreciation of evidence-- Eye-witnesses were reliable and trustworthy-- No delay in F.I.R.-- Previous enmity--Resident of same village-- Consideration of--Held-- As the eye-witnesses have fully supported the prosecution--More or so the fact that witnesses of extra judicial confession or recovery of weapon etc. did not support the prosecution would not detract from their evidence--Order of acquittal is against the evidence on record--Set aside--Convicted the accused under Section 302 I.P.C.--Appeal allowed.

Brief Facts:

i. M. Narasimha Rao, the respondent herein, and the deceased T. Subbaiah were residents of village Veknuru. The deceased was married with PW2 and they had two sons PWs.1 and 3. Some two months prior to the present incident, a quarrel had taken place between the respondent and PW1 in which PW1 had suffered a beating. In order to avenge this insult, PW3 went to the house of the respondent and gave him a sound thrashing. On 13th September 1995, PW3 planned to go on a religious journey to Pedakakani and while doing so, he requested his mother 2PW2 and his father to sleep in his house while he was away. Accordingly, the deceased and PW2 went to the house of PW3 to sleep there that night. At about mid night on the night intervening between 13th and 14th September 1995, the accused respondent reached the house of PW3 armed with a knife and on seeing a person sleeping on the cot in the verandah, and believing him to be PW3, attacked him administering several knife blows. On hearing the commotion, PW2 who was sleeping on a mat besides her husband's cot, cried out in alarm and also attempted to intervene to save her husband, but the accused pushed her down. In the meanwhile, PW1 whose house was close by also rushed to spot and he also witnessed the incident and attempted to catch the accused who, however, managed to run away. The accused thereafter went to the house of his maternal uncle PW6 who told him to get out of the house. At 8 a.m. on 14th September 1995 PW1 went to the Village Administrative Officer PW8 and narrated the incident to him. PW8 recorded the circumstances in writing and sent the information to Police Station Avanigadda and a formal FIR was registered in the Police Station. The accused was thereafter arrested and on the completion of the investigation, a charge sheet was filed under Sections 449 and 302 of the IPC. He pleaded false implication and claimed trial. In support of its case, prosecution examined 13 witnesses in all, the primary witnesses, being one PW1, the elder son of the deceased, who had come to the place of incident during the occurrence after hearing cries of his mother and had also attempted to apprehend him, PW2, the wife of the deceased and mother of PW1 and PW3, the younger brother of PW1, who had gone on a pilgrimage and was in fact the cause of the attack and PW8 the Village Administrative Officer, who had recorded the first information report. Certain other witnesses, who are not eye witnesses, were, however, declared hostile. The prosecution also relied upon various documents such as the post-mortem report and circumstantial evidence such as the recovery of the murder weapon at the instance of the accused etc. The trial court relying on the evidence of PW1 and PW2, both eye witnesses, and the closest relatives of the deceased, as corroborated by the statement of PW3 with regard to the motive convicted the accused. It held that though some of the witness had not supported the prosecution story, it was of no consequence as they had no role to play in determining the truthfulness of the eye witness account of PW1 and PW2. The court accordingly held that though PWs 6 and 9 with respect to the extra judicial confession and the recovery of weapon of murder had not supported the prosecution , this factor would have no effect on the prosecution story. The court also observed that in the light of the fact that the incident had happened at night and PW2 was an old woman 75 years of age and must have been completely traumatized by the events, the mere fact that the FIR had been lodged at about 10 a.m. or the special report had been delivered four hours later, could not detract from the prosecution story. The trial court, accordingly, convicted and sentenced the accused to undergo imprisonment for life under Section 302 of the IPC but did not record any conviction under Section 449 of the IPC. An appeal was thereafter taken to the High Court of the State of Andhra Pradesh. The Division Bench by its judgment dated 18th April 2002 reversed the findings of the trial court and acquitted the accused. In doing so, the High Court observed that as some of the witnesses, PWs.4, 5, and 6, who had reached the place of incident soon after the incident, had turned hostile and PW9, the witness of the extra judicial confession had also not supported the prosecution, the reliance on the statements of PWs.1 and 2 alone was a matter which needed examination with care. It observed that PW2 was the wife of the deceased and was an eye witness but as PW1 had come to the spot after the occurrence and had not been present at the time of the incident, it appeared 5[th]at he was not an eye-witness, and the court had to be extremely careful before recording a verdict of guilt on the basis of the statement of a solitary witness. The court then held that the incident had been happened at about mid night of the 13th and 14th September and the FIR had been lodged after 8 hours though the Police Station was 7 km. away from the place of incident and in the fact that the special report had been delivered 4 hours later to the Magistrate's Court, which was in the same compound as the Police Station was also belated exercise. The present appeal has been filed by the State of Andhra Pradesh challenging the order of the High Court and after the grant of leave, the matter is before us.

ii. The learned Counsel for the appellant has, first and foremost, pointed out that there was no reason whatsoever to disbelieve PW1 and PW2 as they were eye witnesses to the incident and also the closest relatives of the deceased. It has been further pointed out that only witnesses, who could be expected at the night in a residential house, would be the immediate members of the family and to look for evidence beyond these witnesses was difficult to accept. It has also been pleaded that there was no delay in the lodging the FIR as the statement had been made by PW2 to the Village Administrative Officer at about 8 a.m. and it was his duty to forward the information to the Police Station and if in doing so, some time had been taken as the Police Station was 7 km. away from the village, there was absolutely no delay in registration of the FIR. It has been further submitted that the delay in the delivery of the special report would become insignificant in the light of the categoric eye witness evidence.

Held, while convicting the accused:

We are also of the opinion that there is no delay in the recording of the FIR. It cannot be ignored that PW2 had witnessed the murder of her husband and that too in a most brutal and bloodcurdling manner as the evidence is that the injuries had led to a huge amount of bleeding. PW-2 was a lady of 75 years of age but she had nevertheless given the statement to the Village Administrative Officer at about 8 a.m. and the information had been forwarded to the police station. If any delay occurred after 8 a.m. it was a matter which was beyond the control of PW2. In any case, in the light of the fact that information had been conveyed to the police station at 10 a.m. of what had happened at 1 or 2 a.m. in a remote village 7 km. away from the police station, we are of the opinion that there was no delay in the lodging of the FIR and if there was some delay, it stood explained. In the face of unimpeachable evidence the late delivery of the special report by itself would do no great damage to the prosecution story. We, accordingly, allow this appeal, set aside the judgment of the High Court and convict the accused respondent under Section 302 of the IPC and sentence him to undergo RI for life and a fine of Rs. 100/- and in default of fine, to undergo SI for 15 days. The accused respondent be taken into custody forthwith to serve out his sentence.

CHAPTER TWENTY

State of H.P. Vs. Ram Krishan, 2009

Hon'ble Judges/Coram:

Dr. Arijit Pasayat and Mukundakam Sharma, JJ.

Equivalent Citation: 2009(1)ACR494(SC), 2009(74)AIC17, 2009 (64) ACC 632, 2009(1)ALT(Cri)345, 2009((1))ALT(Cri)345, 2009CriLJ1138, JT2009(1)SC344, 2009(5)RCR(Criminal)793, 2009(1)SCALE324, (2009)11SCC327, [2009]1SCR132, MANU/SC/0021/2009

Relevant Section: Sections 302 of the Indian Penal Code, 1860

Number of Pages in the Original Judgment: 03

Case Note:

Indian Penal Code, 1860 - Section 302--Murder--Acquittal by High Court--Whether justified?--Held, "no"--Eye-witnesses stated that accused hit deceased on left side of head with stone--And he rolled down--Deceased died of head injury--No material before High Court for conclusion that death occurred due to fall--High Court's order based on conjectures and surmises--Unsustainable and set aside--Order of conviction recorded by trial court restored.

Brief Facts:

Laxmi Dutt (PW-1), resident of village Mandap in Tehsil Karsog was running a tailoring shop at the material time in village Maghundi at a distance of about one kilometer from his residential house. Manohar Lal (hereinafter referred to as the 'deceased') was his younger brother and was running a shop of general merchandise at Maghandi in the business premises of PW-1 in the morning and evening, while during the day time he used to teach students of a nearby school. On 26.11.1998 at about 7.30 p.m. when the deceased was present in his aforesaid business premises, Ram Krishan (hereinafter referred to as the 'accused') and Harmender

Singh (hereafter referred to as 'the co-accused') came there while under the influence of liquor. They wanted to take more liquor at the said business premises of the deceased. They asked the deceased to give them some eatables. The deceased, however, asked the accused persons not to take liquor in his business premises which infuriated them and as a result they quarrelled with the deceased and slapped him. The accused persons also threw the goods at the business premises of the deceased helter-skelter. When the deceased asked them not to indulge in such mischief, they asked him to get lost. Thereupon the deceased went to the houses of Pawan Kumar (PW-5) and Dogar Ram residents of village Thaltu. The deceased informed them about the acts and conduct of the accused persons and then returned to his business premises along with PW5 and Dogar Ram, who is elder brother of accused Harmender Singh. PW-5 and Dogar Ram requested the accused persons not to commit the mischief in the business premises of the deceased. However, the accused persons asked them to get lost. The deceased then went to his house and informed Laxmi Dutt (PW-1) and Karam Dass (PW 6) and other persons present in the house about the acts and conduct of the accused persons. Laxmi Dutt (PW-1), Amba Dutt (PW2), Nanak Chand (PW3) and Preen Lal came along with the deceased and reached the business premises at about 8.15 p.m. They inquired from the accused persons as to why they had picked up a quarrel with the deceased? On such enquiry, the accused persons stepped out of the business premises of Manohar Lal (deceased), and with a stone, hit on the left side of his head and as a consequence, the deceased dropped dead at the site where he had sustained injury with stone Ext. P-1 and rolled down the hill-side upto a distance of about 50 feet. The accused persons thereafter pelted stones on the other persons present there thereby causing simple hurt to PW6 and Dogar Ram. On hearing the noise from the spot, Man Singh (PW7) also came to the place of occurrence. He asked the accused persons not to pelt stones and took them to their houses. PW-1, PW-7 and Khuba Raid went to the house of Krishna Devi (PW-4), Pardhan of the Gram Panchayat and informed her of the murder of Manohar Lal (deceased). She accompanied them to the place of occurrence and inspected the dead body of the deceased. Thereafter, PW-1, PW-4 and PW-7 went to Police Station, Karsog and lodged FIR. Ext. PW-1/A under Sections 452, 323, 427, 302/34 of the Indian Penal Code against the accused persons and the investigation in the matter followed. SHO, Harbhajan Singh, S.I. (PW-13) visited the place of occurrence and took the dead body of Manohar Lal in possession.

Photographs of the dead body and the place of occurrence were taken and the developed photographs are Exts. PW-10/A-1 to PW-10/A-8. The report Marg Exts. PW-13/B and PW-13/C were prepared and the dead body was sent for post mortem examination. Stone Ext. PW 1 was also taken in possession vide recovery memo. Ext.PW-4/1 and was sealed. Stone Ext. P2 was also taken in possession from the business premises of the deceased vide recovery memo Ext. PW-4/B. The post mortem of the dead body of the deceased was conducted by Dr. Girish (PW-14) and the post mortem report issued by him is Ext. PW-14/A. As per opinion of PW- 14, the deceased died due to the injuries to brain caused by the head injury.

Held, while allowing the appeal:

The High Court's conclusion is that no one examined the body of the deceased before it rolled down to ascertain whether he was alive or dead. It is relevant that all the eye witnesses had stated about the assault of the head of the deceased by the accused with the stone. Injury No. 9 was described as the fatal injury; At least five of the injuries were on the head, which can be related to the assault by the stone and more particularly injury No. 9 viz. the fracture in the left temporal region. Since the High Court's order is based on surmises and conjectures, it cannot be sustained and is set aside and the order of conviction recorded by the trial court stands restored. The respondent shall surrender to custody forthwith to serve remainder of sentence.

Appeal is allowed to the aforesaid extent.

Videos & Tv Shows On Law & Exim

List of some important videos & TV shows on Law & EXIM by Adv. Jayprakash Somani on his YouTube Channel 'Jayprakash Somani EXIM & Legal'

Legal Videos: Hindi -English

1) SLP in Supreme Court / Special Leave Petitions in the Supreme Court of India

2) Transfer of Civil & Criminal Cases by the Supreme Court of India / Transfer of Matrimonial Cases

3) Appellate Jurisdiction of the Supreme Court of India

4) Jurisdictions of the Supreme Court of India

5) Public Interest Litigation in the Supreme Court of India / PIL in Supreme Court

6) Article 32 Writ Petitions in the Supreme Court of India

7) Bail Matters Top 10 Supreme Court Cases

8) FIR Quashing in High Court & Supreme Court

9) Bail & Anticipatory Bail Matters in Supreme Court

10) Insolvency & Bankruptcy Matters in the Supreme Court

11) Insolvency & Bankruptcy Code 2016 Part 1

12) Insolvency & Bankruptcy Code 2016 Part 2

13) Insolvency & Bankruptcy Code 2016 Part 3

14) Corporate Liquidation Process

15) Supreme Court Rules & Procedures Webinar of 2.5 hour on Zoom

16) RDDBFI Act, 1993 (Introduction)

17) The Indian Contact Act 1872

18) Negotiable Instruments Act (Introduction)

19) How to avoid matrimonial disputes& some more videos

20) SEBI Matters in the Supreme Court

21) Matrimonial Matters: Supreme Court's 20 Case Laws

22) Consumer Matters Supreme Court's 20 Case Laws

23) Service Matters Supreme Court's 20 Case Laws

24) How to Search Lawyer for Your Matter

25) Property Matters Supreme Court's 20 Case Laws

26) Bail Matters: Supreme Court's 20 Case Laws

27) Supreme Court / High Court Vacation Benches

28) 69000 Teacher's Recruitment Matters of UP Government in the Supreme Court

29) Contempt of Court Matters in the Supreme Court

30) Advocate Act's Matters in the Supreme Court

31) Business Law Matters in the Supreme Court

32) Banking Matters in the Supreme Court

33) Labour Law Matters in the Supreme Court

34) Arbitration Matters in the Supreme Court

35) Careers in Law -Zoom Webinar by Adv. Jayprakash Somani

36) Civil Matters in the Supreme Court

37) Consumer Protection Act | Consumer Matters in the Supreme Court

38) Corporate Matters in the Supreme Court

39) Criminal Matters in the Supreme Court

40) Role of Respondent in the Supreme Court of India

41) Motor Vehicle Accident Matters in Supreme Court with case laws

42) Article 131 Original Suits in Supreme Court

43) PIL in Supreme Court/ Public Interest Litigations in the Supreme Court of India'

44) CAB Citizenship Amendment Bill is not Unconstitutional

45) Supreme Court of India Cases & Process – Marathi

46) Legal Services Export / Export of Legal Services

47) Transfer of Matrimonial Cases by the Supreme Court of India

48) Public Interest Litigation PIL

49) The Specific Relief Act (Introduction)

50) Corporate Insolvency Resolution Process CIRP

51) ABMM's Career 5 - Careers in Law

52) Transfer of cases by Supreme Court

53) Writ Petitions in High Court & Supreme Court of India

54) Supreme Court Jurisdictions - Appeals, SLP, Writ Petitions, Transfer, Original, Review, Curative

55) LEGAL INDIA TV Show: Cases Handled in Supreme Court

56) Corporate Liquidation Process

57) Legal Services Export / Export of Legal Services

58) Corporate Laws

59) Election Matters- Supreme Court's 20 Case Laws

60) Companies Act, 2013

62) Competition Act, 2002

63) Banking Matters - Supreme Court's 20 Case Laws

64) Election Matters in the Supreme Court

65) Armed Forces Tribunal Matters in the Supreme Court

66) Compassionate Appointment Service matter

67) Foreign Exchange Management Act FEMA

68) Foreign Trade Policy 2021-26 Proposed

69) Customs Act 1962

70) Narcotic Drugs and Psychotropic Substances Act, 1985 NDPS Act

71) Foreign Trade Development & Regulation Act, 1992

72) How to Search Good Advocate in the Supreme Court of India

73) Sr. Adv Vikas Singh's Interview in Nani Palkhivala Wednesday Law Club

EXIM Videos: Hindi -English

1) Yes, I can do Import Export Business Easily! 36 points excellent video in Hindi

2) Yes, I can do Import Export Business Easily! 36 points excellent video in English

3) Import Export Business – Hindi video

4) Import Export Business - English video

5) Export Import Marathi TV Interview

6) Scope for Commerce Students in International Business- TV Show

7) Scope for Management Student in International Business- TV Show

8) Scope for Engineering Students in International Business – TV Show

9) Women in International Business- TV Show

10) How to do Import Export Business Successfully!'

11) Where one can get full information on Import Export Business?

12) What to do import & export?

13) Import Export Workshop/ Training/Course/ Diploma

14) How to Start Import Export Business & How to grow it. Live Webinar

15) Success Stories & Failure Stories in Import & Export Business

16) For MSME Scope in Export & Import...

17) Exports In Agri. & Food Products – English & some more videos

18) Exports to Dubai, Aabudhabii. e. UAE

19) Jewellery Exports from India

20) How to attend EXIM workshop to become excellent Exporter

21) Import Export Best Training Course – Online & Offline

22) Agri Product Export

23) Scope for Woman in International Business

24) Management Graduates Scope in International Business

25) Pharma Product's Export

26) Best Import Export Course | Practical Training | Aaronica Global Exim

27) Import Export Business for Commerce Graduates

28) How Do I Get Export Orders? Finding International Buyers

29) What Is APEDA In Import Export Business?

30) Which Is The Best Product To Export From India?

31) EXIM Remark by Manoj Kumar Faridabad

32) EXIM Remarks by Mahesh Telangana

33) What Licenses I Need To Start Import/ Export?

34) How Can I Increase My Import Export Business?

35) Which Is Best B2B Website For Import/Export Business?

36) Export Import Management with Global Marketing

37) How to Start Export Import Business | 51 Points Video

38) Scope for Commerce & Other Graduates in International Business

39) BE A SUCCESSFUL EXPORTER FOR OUR NATION - Marathi video

40) Export of Textile , Cotton, Agri., Food, & other products & services

41) Exports from MP, CG, MH, GJ & CA in Fresh Fruits & Vegetables

42) Exports in Agri. & Food Products- Hindi

43) Start your Online/E-Commerce Business

44) How to Start Export Import Business & Grow it

45) Exports in Textile & Other Products

46) Start and grow EXIM business - Live English Webinar

47)'Import Export Business!' Why, Who, What & How can one do it easily!!

48) Live: Export of Product & Services During & After Lock Down Period

49) Frauds in Import Export Business

50) Import Export for Business Man

51) Import & Export for Women

51) Import & Export for Graduate & Post - Graduate Students

52) Agriculture Exports from India

53) Digital Marketing Setup - Marathi

54) 2nd Secret of Successful Businessman

55) Digital Marketing Set up

56) Legal Services Export / Export of Legal Services

57) Export & Import with UAE

58) Service Exports / Exports by Service Providers

59) Import Export Workshop/ Training/Course/ Diploma

60) Exports & Imports with USA

61) Selection on Product for Export

62) Top Products Exported from India

63) What to do import & export?

64) ABMM Career 2 - 'Careers in Business & Industries

65) How to do Import Export Business Successfully!'

66) 5 Secrets of Successful Businessman

67) Export from MP, Chhattisgarh & Vidarbha Nagpur

68) EXIM Hindi - Textile & Apparel Export

69) EXIM Hindi - Export Import Practical Training In Delhi, Kolkata, Mumbai and Pune

70) Import Export Business

71) Import Export Business Hindi

72) Import Export Business English video

73) Import Export Business Marathi

74) Women in International Business by Exim Guru Adv. Jayprakash Somani

75) Opportunities in Foreign Trade- Adv. Jayprakash Somani's special interview

76) Textile Exports

77) India's Number in Exports. How to improve it?

78) 11 Benefits of Exim Workshop

79) Export Import Management with Global Marketing- 13 days Training Workshop

80) Cosmetic's Export

82) Export After COVID

83) Spices Exports

84) Handicraft Export

85) 10 Products India Exports to the World

List Of Adv. Jayprakash Somani's Books

1. Supreme Court of India's Leading Case Laws on 'Insolvency & Bankruptcy Code 2016'
2. Bail Matters – Supreme Court's Latest Leading Case Laws
3. Arbitration Matters- Supreme Court's Latest Leading Case Laws
4. Property Matters - Supreme Court's Latest Leading Case Laws
5. Matrimonial Matters- Supreme Court's Latest Leading Case Laws
6. Election Matters- Supreme Court's Latest Leading Case Laws
7. SEBI Matters- Supreme Court's Latest Leading Case Laws
8. Banking Matters- Supreme Court's Latest Leading Case Laws
9. Service Matters- Supreme Court's Latest Leading Case Laws
10. Contempt of Court Matters- Supreme Court's Latest Leading Case Laws
11. Consumer Protection Matters- Supreme Court's Latest Leading Case Laws
12. Corporate Law- Supreme Court's Latest Leading Case Laws
13. Supreme Court's AOR Exam- Leading Cases
14. Armed Force Tribunal - Supreme Court's Latest Leading Case Laws
15. Acquittal From 376 - Supreme Court's Latest Leading Case Laws
16. Negotiable instrument – Supreme Court's Latest Leading Case Laws
17. Contract Act- Supreme Court's Latest Leading Case Laws
18. Insider trading- Supreme Court's Latest Leading Case Laws
19. Foreign Exchange and Management Act- Supreme Court's Latest Leading Case Laws
20. Income Tax Act- Supreme Court's Latest Leading Case Laws
21. Company Law- Supreme Court's Latest Leading Case Laws
22. Competition & Monopoly Matters- Supreme Court's Latest Leading Case Laws
23. Compassionate Appointment- Service Matters- Supreme Court's Latest Leading Case Laws
24. Compulsory Retirement- Service Matters- Supreme Court's Latest Leading Case Laws
25. Voluntary Retirement- Service Matters- Supreme Court's Latest Leading Case Laws

26. Removal/Dismissal/Termination from Service- Supreme Court's Latest Leading Case Laws

27. Seniority- Service Matter- Supreme Court's Latest Leading Case Laws

28. Promotion- Service Matter- Supreme Court's Latest Leading Case Laws

29. Equal Pay for Equal Work- Service Matter- Supreme Court's Latest Leading Case Laws

30. Condition of Service- Service Matter- Supreme Court's Latest Leading Case Laws

31. Customs Act- Supreme Court's Leading Case Laws

32. Information Technology Act- Supreme Court's Leading Case Laws

33. SEC. 125 CR. P. C.- Supreme Court's Leading Case Laws

34. SEC. 498A OF I. P. C.- Supreme Court's Leading Case Laws

35. MOTOR VEHICLE ACT- Supreme Court's Leading Case Laws

36. CONDITION OF SERVICE- SERVICE MATTER- Supreme Court's Leading Case Laws

37. SUSPENSION- SERVICE MATTER- Supreme Court's Leading Case Laws

38. Reservation in SC, ST, OBC- Service Matter- Supreme Court's Leading Case Laws

39. NARCOTIC DRUGS AND PSYCHOTROPIC SUBSTANCES (NDPS) ACT - Supreme Court of India's Latest Leading Case Laws

40. SEC 302 IPC - Supreme Court of India's Latest Leading Case Laws

Books are available online in India

1. **Notion Press:** https://notionpress.com/author/jayprakash_somani

2. **Amazon:** https://www.amazon.in/s?k=jayprakash+somani

3. **Flipkart:** https://www.flipkart.com/search?q=Jayprakash%20Somani

Books are available online at International Market

4. **Amazon International:** https://www.amazon.com/s?k=jayprakash+somani

5. **Amazon United Kingdom:** https://www.amazon.co.uk/s?k=jayprakash+somani

6. **E-Books/Kindle edition at National & International Level:** https://www.amazon.in/s?k=jaypraksh+somani

www.ingramcontent.com/pod-product-compliance
Lightning Source LLC
Chambersburg PA
CBHW050606160726
48003CB00003B/1071